SECOND EDITION

THE SMALL BUSINESS LIFE CYCLE

THE NO-FLUFF GUIDE TO NAVIGATING THE FIVE STAGES OF **SMALL BUSINESS GROWTH**

D1556371

CHARLIE GILKEY

CONTENTS

INTRODUCTION

This book discusses the unique life cycle of small businesses—including microbusinesses and online businesses—and while you might find this to be interesting information, you may wonder why it's valuable and relevant. It's simple, really: the more you understand where your business is, the more you can focus on taking meaningful action on the stuff that matters for your business now.

I've worked with and taught many hundreds of entrepreneurs and small business owner-executives, and I've seen most of them feel overwhelmed by all the information they get about how to grow their businesses. One expert says one thing and another says something else. Best practices from last year are obsolete this year. And there's always more to do than time and resources available to do it with.

This book will help you determine which information is relevant to you and what steps are right for you to take now. You'll be able to put some things in the "implement now" bucket and put other things in the "implement later" bucket—and, better still, you'll see what you don't need to implement at all.

If you're relatively early in your entrepreneurial journey and none of that makes sense, that's okay, too. You rightly have other concerns that we'll address in the first few chapters.

Before we dive into talking more about how small businesses grow, I'd like to tell a quick story.

About two years ago, I accidentally discovered that I love guacamole. We'll set aside the mystery of how it took me thirty-two years to make this discovery, given that I spent twenty-two of those years eating and loving Mexican food and that I worked in a TexMex restaurant as a teenager; guacamole was green with a weird consistency and I wanted nothing to do with it until my happy accident. The restaurant where I made the discovery makes the guacamole right at the table, and after seeing it made a few times, I decided that I was done paying $8 for guacamole and that I'd make it at home. The restaurant had shown me the ingredients and the process, so surely I could do it myself. Additionally, my wife had started making it and keeping the ingredients stocked, so all I had to do was do what Angela and the restaurant servers did.

If you've never made guacamole or seen it made, you need to know that the basic ingredients of guacamole are avocado, tomatoes, onions, cilantro, and lime (store-bought pico de gallo can be substituted for the tomatoes, onions, and cilantro). There's no cooking involved. In other words, it consists of five basic ingredients and a little bit of mashing and stirring; it's not exactly rocket science.

One day I had a particularly bad craving for guacamole and I knew that *that* was the day I'd establish my guacamole independence. I mentally replayed the technique I'd seen, gathered all of the ingredients, and proceeded to cut the avocado in half and pull the pit out of the middle. I diligently grabbed the spoon to get the avocado meat out of the fruit, expecting it to pop right out like it did for the servers at the restaurant.

Much to my surprise, the meat did *not* pop right out and instead bent the spoon. I improvised by grabbing a knife to see if I could cut the meat out, to no avail. I improvised yet again and got an apple peeler so I could eliminate the rind of the avocado and just focus on smashing the meat of it.

Once I was working with just the inside of the avocado, I tried to smash it again with the spoon, to no avail. I grabbed a larger masher and still didn't get anywhere. So I started slicing and chopping the insides into smaller pieces to see if that would help. It did not.

I was not going to let this avocado beat me. I have moved battalions, commanded a company of soldiers, and coordinated joint-force military operations. I'm finishing up a PhD in Philosophy. I've grown a website into a full-fledged international consulting and education company. Guacamole is five $%^$ ingredients, with the foundation of it being a mashed avocado, and I *knew* how to do it.

I eventually put the avocado in a food processor to chop it up into fine pieces so I could mash it again. The processed avocado still did not yield to my demands to be mashed. In a fit of exasperation, I combined the remaining ingredients and began eating this amalgam that tasted like guacamole but did not look or feel like guacamole. I had not spent the past forty-five minutes of my life battling an avocado to walk away with nothing.

As I was eating my salsamole, my wife came home and saw my crazed expression. She looked at what I was eating, reviewed the sprawl of kitchen tools that were out, and gave me the "what happened here?" look that only partners can give each other, so I began to explain my ordeal. I ended with "I did it just like I saw and I have no idea why it was so hard to do."

She chuckled and told me that the avocado wasn't ripe yet. She was planning on using it later in the week and had bought it before it was ripe so that it wouldn't be over-ripe by the time she was going to use it.

I tell this story because it's similar to what happens for many founders and small business owners. They "learn" how to do it, they assemble all of the right ingredients, and many months or years later, they're exhausted but unwilling to give up. Their struggles are often just a result of their not working on the right things at the right time—the avocado that is their business, market, product, or team just isn't ripe yet.

My sincere hope is that this book gets you to focus on the opportunities and challenges you're ripe for and avoid the hard work of attempting to mash an avocado that just isn't ready to be mashed.

One Size Doesn't Fit All—And Businesses Grow Differently

The main premise of this book is that small businesses have a unique life cycle that's different from the life cycles of corporations, funded startups, franchises, and so on. I often do translate the schema in this book into those other types of businesses to give you clear examples, but I want to keep the focus on small businesses. After all, about 90 percent of all businesses fall within the small business category.

The chief reason that small businesses have a different life cycle is that so many of them are bootstrapped, with little to no upfront capital. Bootstrapped businesses have the huge advantage of being customer-focused out of necessity, but at the same time, their growth comes from what they pull in—and a growing business is a hungry business. So much of the early-stage resources are put into the day-to-day hustle that there's rarely any left over for strategic investments in the people, processes, systems, and positioning needed to get out of this early-stage hustle.

The result of this continual bootstrapping is that the pain of not having the right people, processes, systems, and positioning in place shows up much later in bootstrapped businesses' life cycle. These inefficiencies, misalignments, and over-taxed people prevent the business from moving forward. You'll learn more about this in Chapter 4.

If the last two paragraphs hit home for you, it's okay. You haven't done anything wrong; in fact, you've done a phenomenal job—so few businesses actually get to that point in the first place because they don't make it through the Entry and Growth stages. You're sitting on a powder keg of possibilities.

An Overview of the Stages of the Small Business Life Cycle

Every stage of business has its own challenges, strengths, inconvenient truths, ways forward, and catalytic moments. There are no free lunches here, and no matter how cool it is to look from here at how much you want to be *there*—wherever "there" is—understand that once you get there, you will still have challenges.

If you've read Martha Beck's *Finding Your Own North Star*, you'll see many parallels. I had been working with the ideas in this model for a while with my clients and friends, and Martha's framework crystallized it into something more concrete.

There are five distinct stages in the small business life cycle. I'll start with a picture and then move to a brief overview:

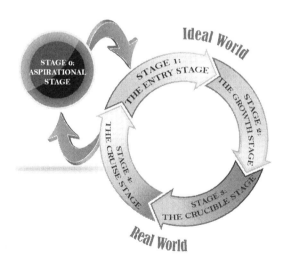

- **Stage 0—the Aspirational stage.** People in this stage want to start a business and like the idea of it, but they haven't committed to becoming entrepreneurs.

- **Stage 1—the Entry stage.** People in this stage have decided to start a business and are actively building their market and offers. They might not have many or any customers, but they're no longer sitting on the fence about being an entrepreneur.

- **Stage 2—the Growth stage.** Entrepreneurs in this stage have a business plan and are growing their revenue streams with new clients and customers. These entrepreneurs aren't booked solid or running at full capacity yet, but there's no longer a question that they have a viable business model.

- **Stage 3—the Crucible stage.** Entrepreneurs in this stage are at the delightfully frustrating point at which they're booked solid and working at full steam, but the demand for their goods and services outstrips their ability to meet it. Something has to give, but entrepreneurs often don't want to let go of the business activities that have gotten them to this stage.

- **Stage 4—the Cruise stage.** Entrepreneurs in this stage have figured out what it was that kept them bottlenecked and constricted at Stage 3, have fixed it, and are now running full steam ahead. They have the team and support they need in order to focus on their core competencies, or if they don't, they have a specific plan in place to get those resources.

So how do the ideal world and the real world differ? In Stages 0, 1, and 2, entrepreneurs are working in a world of their own imagining—the constraints of reality either have to be discounted or aren't real and pressing problems. For instance, many

Stage 1 and early Stage 2 businesses do fine without complex accounting systems because they're simple enough that it's not a real problem. However, in Stage 3, percentages, margins, and partner distributions make big differences to the daily operations of the business and to the people who own and run them. At the tail end of Stage 4, new possibilities and uncharted territories that seem new, fun, cool, or interesting mask the reality under them, so many an entrepreneur is lured back into Stage 1.

The stark differences between the ideal world and the real world are the chief reason these stages constitute a cycle rather than a straight linear progression. At Stage 4, entrepreneurs tend to do one of three things.

1. Implement a new business model or brand dynamic. For instance, entrepreneurs might write books and become public speakers, in which case they have to start all over again because the business path for public speakers is dramatically different from the entrepreneurs' old path. Or they might franchise their business model or ideas, leading to increased revenue but also to unique challenges.

2. Lose a critical resource in their current business. Perhaps a competitor unexpectedly outcompetes them, resulting in the loss of revenue due to lost market share, or their Chief Operations Officer dies or leaves the company. This might not bump entrepreneurs down to Stage 0 or 1, but it definitely might hamper their ability to deliver solutions to their customers or clients. (Think of what happened to Yahoo when Google hit the scene.)

3. Sell the current business, only to start another. Some entrepreneurs are serial entrepreneurs by choice, building sellable businesses by design. Others are serial entrepreneurs by accident—they sell their business for whatever reason, only to find themselves unexpectedly bored, excited, or ready to do it again.

Another reason these stages constitute a life cycle is that in the entrepreneurial world, we'll often do things that change our position and start the cycle anew. For example, we might be in Stage 3 and have a lucky break. We'll present a new offer or start a new business that gets us back in the Growth stage, but we still haven't fundamentally fixed whatever had us stuck in Stage 3. Generally, it's harder to move up and stay up than it is to move back down the cycle and stay there.

Where This Model Gets Tricky

If you're a serial entrepreneur who is running multiple businesses simultaneously, you may have a hard time placing yourself in a stage because your businesses are at different levels of growth. In this case, it's best to default to your own capacity when deciding what you need in order to enable more simultaneous business growth. That said, your individual businesses may have different needs than you do. For instance, a new business venture may need its brand to be established, but that brand is distinct from your personal brand as an entrepreneur. The farther apart the two are, the more you'll have to separate what the business needs for growth versus what you need for growth.

Or you may be someone who has difficulty separating your holistic personal life cycle from your entrepreneurial life cycle. You see this when entrepreneurs develop a lot of experience, confidence, and skills as employees and then become entrepreneurs. While you can map employee experience over to entrepreneurial experience, it can be tricky. Many experienced former employees spend a lot of time beating themselves up for having to learn so many of the entrepreneurial lessons they thought they would know already.

(If this is you, it's okay that you are where you are. You couldn't have seen the reality that you're living now, so the sooner you embrace the learning opportunity and challenges, the easier it'll be to build some momentum and start flourishing.)

Wherever You Are, It's Okay

The grass is always greener on the other side of the fence, and this is never more true than in small business. We think that if we just make it to the next stage, all of our problems will go away.

What we often forget is that even though the grass may be greener on the other side, it still needs mowing. The next stage in a business cycle will present different challenges, and your task will always be to assess the resources you have now and productively use them to solve the challenges of the day.

You don't want your business to run out of problems and challenges because that means either you're out of business or you're asleep at the wheel. You want different and better challenges tomorrow than you have today; if you've been solving the same problem for the past few years, it's time to reevaluate your approach to solving that problem.

Every stage has virtues worth celebrating. The possibilities and excitement of Stage 0, the courage to start and get into Stage 1, the thrill of the home run at Stage 2, the great problem of having demand outstrip capacity in Stage 3, or the steady predictability and control of Stage 4—no single virtue is better than the others, and they all play a part.

Wherever you are, it's okay. If you can't confidently and powerfully stand where you are, neither will you be able to confidently and powerfully take the next step or stand firm if you take that step.

"A journey of a thousand miles starts with one step" is often attributed to Lao Tzu, author of the *Tao Te Ching*. A better interpretation is "a journey of a thousand miles begins beneath the feet." The difference: the latter acknowledges that you're already on the journey, rather than assuming that the journey starts when you take the step.

And since you've already started the journey that is this book, let's move on to the next chapter. Before you do, though, I want to thank you for being in business and for supporting me by buying, reading, or sharing this book.

CHAPTER ONE
Stage 0: The Aspirational Stage

"Whenever you see a successful business,
someone once made a courageous decision."
—Peter Drucker

Stage 0—the Aspirational stage—is a logical placeholder for all the people who want to start a business. They read books about business, or they sit in school dreaming about starting a business, but they haven't actually started one yet.

Challenges of Stage 0

One of the main challenges is an extension of Barry Schwartz's insight from his book, *The Paradox of Choice*, that shows that having more choices often leads to less choosing. Having so many possibilities around what business you *could* start can make it harder for you to choose *which* business to start.

The second challenge of the Aspirational stage is making the leap from the status quo. Making that leap is hard. People will tell you that it's better to keep your job. They don't understand what you're doing, especially if you already have a good job at a place like Google or another one of the whiz-bang companies that everyone wants to work for. The idea of jumping out and starting your own business is ludicrous to many people. Trying to buck the status quo is a huge challenge if you're still shaky and lacking the confidence for starting a business.

The third challenge of Stage 0 is the enormity of changing the world. Everything is so big. Not only are there so many different ways to start a business, but you're also thinking about the kind of mark you're trying to make in the universe. The enormity of changing the world can be so big that people decide they don't have it in them to do it, and so they don't.

Strengths of Stage 0

One of the strengths of Stage 0 is that you still have hope. You haven't been burned, you haven't had a slump month, season, or year, and you haven't invested months and many thousands of dollars in something only to have it crash in a blaze of publicly humiliating glory. You still have pure, unadulterated hope—and hope is a powerful thing.

Because you haven't started, you have a lot of energy. You haven't walked the road of entrepreneurship and business building yet and thus aren't tired.

Another strength—and it's such a precious thing—is that anything counts as a win. Any advance you have in your business, any hint of interest, anything that gets you money or helps you see that your idea might work counts as a win.

The Inconvenient Truth

There's an inconvenient truth at Stage 0, and this truth keeps people in Stage 0. That inconvenient truth is that your business might not work. Whatever the idea, it might not be viable, there might not be a market for it, or you might not have the resources for it. This truth has existed for everyone who has ever started a business.

The Way Ahead

So, what is the way ahead when you're at Stage 0? It's one of those statements that's simple but not easy, and here it is: Just start. Pick an idea that you're really passionate about or that you believe you can help somebody with, and start. It won't be perfect, but it will never be perfect. It may be ungraceful, but that's kind of the point. The only way you can build the business you're thinking about is to start.

Now, I understand that this suggestion is completely unsatisfying if you're in Stage 0 and you're unsure of how to move forward, so I'm going to provide three suggestions that will help orient you as you head towards Stage 1.

1. Start noticing what things make you come alive.

You'll note that I've started with you as the center of your business-building process, and there's a reason for this. Part of the challenge of getting something started is that you look out into the world and you see all sorts of things you might do. That array of choices keeps you from doing something.

When you start with who you actually are and what makes you come alive, that can become an anchor for scaling down all of those possibilities into a smaller subset of things that would be fun to try. Start with the fun things because some parts of the business journey won't be fun.

A fundamental but often unspoken truth about starting your own business is that there are often long grind periods, sometimes without producing any of the results you want. You'll need something to drive you through the uncertainty of making your new business happen. If you focus on those things that make you come alive, it makes the entire process a lot more fun, and it's easier to hang on until you start getting results.

This reminds me of a quote by Arnold J. Toynbee: "The supreme accomplishment is to blur the line between work and play." What things would you do even if you weren't being paid? Guess what? When you're starting your first business, it might be a while before you get paid. So focusing on the things that make you come alive is very helpful in Stage 0.

A second thing to look at, along the same lines, is: what types of things are you natively good at? Now, I want to be careful here because sometimes the thing that you're good at is not something you should do for a living. You may be a trained professional who has spent a long time getting good at something, yet now you've determined that it wasn't really a good fit. So instead of looking at your training or credentials, look back to your teenage years.

For instance, I've always been able to figure stuff out on the fly. I'm really good at walking into a chaotic situation and making sense of it, figuring out what needs to be happening and who needs to be doing what. It may not have seemed like a particularly important skill at the time, but it has turned out to be incredibly valuable in a small business and in an entrepreneurial landscape.

I can walk into a business, start observing and asking questions, and almost immediately be able to figure out what needs to be happening. This ability is really helpful because a lot of people can't do this, certainly not in their own business, and they need somebody to come in and do it for them. In retrospect, it makes sense that I've started the business that I'm in now, but it took me awhile to get here and to see how valuable that skill is in the marketplace. If I'd looked back at what I was good at as a teenager, I would have had a better start.

The last thing to think about in this area of questioning is: who are the people that fire you up? If you have fun with hyper-creative people and they make you come alive, then start figuring out what hyper-creative people need. Maybe you have a lot of fun with amateur chess players. Or perhaps real estate agents are your people. We live in a time in which you don't necessarily need a lot of your right people to have a business working with them; far too many early-stage entrepreneurs cast a net that's too wide rather than too narrow.

2. Look for frustrations you can solve.

Most entrepreneurial businesses get their start because someone is frustrated about the current options available and they decide to do something about it.

Basecamp, the project management software, was created by a team of web designers and developers at 37signals. They didn't like the project solutions available, so they started building their own. They shared these with their clients, and their clients loved them, too. Basecamp began back in the early 2000s and it has evolved into a phenomenal application that makes millions of dollars a year. All because 37signals solved their own frustration.

Solving your own frustration can be risky, but it's also the simplest path to choose because you'll definitely know when you've solved your own problem. You know what the problem feels like and you'll know if the solution works. When you try to solve someone else's frustration, a lot of times you can miss the mark because other people's needs, wants, and aspirations are different from yours, with the result being that you develop a solution that doesn't meet your customers' needs.

Solving a frustration is a solid foundation for a business idea. Listen for people talking about the things that frustrate them—these are important clues for your entrepreneur's ear.

When you combine these explorations of frustrations that you can solve and the things that make you come alive, you can end up in a growth-favoring sweet spot. And that leads to the third way of making it out of Stage 0.

3. Pick one frustration and start generating solutions.

Many people make the mistake here of thinking that they have to come up with big solutions to people's problems, but that's a pathway to a lot of pain in Stage 1. Instead, think about the micro-solutions. What small things could you bring to people's worlds that would solve their pervasive frustration in small ways?

It could be something that's moderately frustrating for a lot of people, or it could be something that's deeply frustrating for a few people. I'm not going to tell you which to choose, but that's something for you to start thinking about. The key point here is that you're developing possible solutions, not that you're coming out of the gate with the right solution. (You'll see why in Stage 3.)

People want to buy small solutions for their problems. Small solutions mean small changes and those are easier for buyers to get their heads around. Most consumers resist solutions that require a massive disruption and instead want simple, easy-to-implement solutions. Granted, there are people who are looking for massive changes in their lives, but most people want change without having to do a lot of work to get it.

Yes, you read that correctly: we want change at the same time that we are resistant to change. It's irrational, and we don't make purchases based on what we think—our most important purchases rest on what we feel. (For more on this, check out Dan Ariely's *Predictably Irrational*.)

Developing simple, doable solutions means that you don't have to fight through your potential buyers' walls of resistance to change.

There's another huge upshot of developing simple, doable solutions: your customers get quick and early wins. If they get quick wins, they're more likely to stick with your business as it grows because they've had a positive experience. The more customers stick with your business, the easier time you'll have making it through Stages 1 and 2.

The Catalytic Moment

A catalytic moment happens here that moves you from Stage 0 to Stage 1. You see some frustration you can solve in the world, you try something, and it works—just a tiny bit. You can see through all the fear and the inconvenient truth, and you think, "Wait a second—there's a possibility here that I can do this." And you start that business.

Stage 0 Summary

- Stage 0 is the Aspirational stage. You're thinking about starting a business or new venture but haven't yet done so.

- The challenges of Stage 0 are that choosing a business can be hard because there are so many possibilities; it's hard to make the leap from having a conventional job to being an entrepreneur; and the idea of changing the world can seem overwhelming.

- The strengths of Stage 0 are that you still have hope; you have a lot of energy; and anything counts as a win.

- The inconvenient truth of Stage 0 is that your idea might not work.

- The ways ahead are to:

  1. Start noticing what makes you come alive, along with what types of things you're natively good at and which kinds of people fire you up.

  2. Look for frustrations you can solve.

  3. Pick one frustration and start generating solutions.

- The catalytic moment that takes you from Stage 0 to Stage 1 occurs when something you try, works; you start to believe that you can do this; and you start that business.

CHAPTER TWO
Stage 1: The Entry Stage

"In the business world, everyone is paid in two coins: cash and experience. Take the experience first; the cash will come later."
—Harold S. Geneen

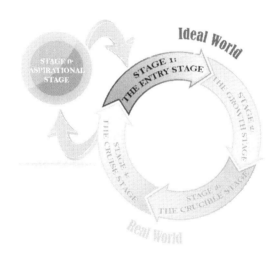

Stage 1 is the Entry stage. This is the stage of business in which you have already started the business. It's already getting a little bit of traction, but you don't yet have a lot of customers, market share, and/or demand for what you do.

Stages 1 and 2 are both "yes" stages. They're yes stages because you say "yes" to a lot. You take on too much; you work with anyone who is willing to work with you, even if they're the wrong people; you say yes to anybody who shows interest in you or anything that seems somewhat relevant. This a natural part of the process.

Challenges of Stage 1

The first challenge is that one lit match does not equal a forest fire. That little success you had in Stage 0 may not take off into something that's sustainable for the long term. It does happen for some people, but it's not common. It's more likely that you started and had a little success, and now you have to light the match all over again. The Entry stage is one of the most awkward stages because you do a lot of small things in the hope that they have bigger effects.

The second challenge of Stage 1 is talking about what you do—also known as marketing. When I'm talking to entrepreneurs and small business owners, I can normally tell how long they've been in business by how long it takes them to tell me what it is they do. Normally, it involves a bunch of unclear statements about what they do and whom they do it with, and it's apparent that they haven't quite nailed down what it is they do and for whom. Because this is a "yes" stage, you try to be inclusive of all possibilities. Your marketing messages tend to be opaque in your quest to be general enough to catch as many different people as possible.

Another challenge is undervaluing what you do. What you do is generally so innate to you, your first thought is that it doesn't have much value. Almost all small businesses start by undervaluing and underpricing their services or products. Undervaluing what you do is a challenge because it's hard to make enough money to have a viable business. Additionally, undervaluing what you do affects your marketing because you can't stand upon the value you provide. It makes it harder for you to advance a compelling reason to work with or buy from you.

Strengths of Stage 1

Let's think about the strengths of Stage 1, though. The first strength is that you still have energy. You're just starting down the road, you're still learning a lot, and there's still a lot of energy to go around. You can build a business at this stage mostly on effort. To parrot Gary Vaynerchuk, you can crush it in Stage 1 because you have the internal resources and the cash flow to back it up.

The second strength is the success high. Every small win gives you a little high because it's still new. The more experience you get at this stage, the happier you are, the more fun it is, and the more it fuels your growth. Small wins count as huge wins to you. For instance, the first time one of your idols links to your blog is a huge deal for you. Later on, it's run of the mill; you lose that joy.

Another strength is that you're not too big to fail. You don't have so many people watching you that failing on stage becomes awkward and the fear of doing so in front of large crowds is even more terrifying. You're not pitching to an audience of thirty thousand people; you're not on national TV having people examine and scrutinize your every word. You're small enough that you can fail, and only eight people plus your cat will know about it. This is a pretty big deal, and this is one of the reasons why other business advocates like Seth Godin advise you to fail fast and fail often.

The more you fail fast and fail often in Stages 1 and 2, the easier it is for you to learn what you need to learn, because in later stages of business, there's more at stake when you fail. You have many more people looking at you, and egos will get involved. I know it sounds odd to say that you're not too big to fail and that you should fail, but that's really one of the blessings of Stage 1.

The Inconvenient Truth

Let's talk about the inconvenient truth of Stage 1: you have no idea what you're doing. You don't have the experience, you don't have the market validation, and you don't understand the business. Even if you've learned about business, learning about business and running your own business are two dramatically different things. In Stage 1, you simply don't know what you're doing. And that's okay.

The Way Ahead

The way ahead in Stage 1 is to refine your products or services.

1. Focus on your beachhead offer.

Your beachhead offer is that one key thing you do to establish a foothold in a marketplace. All too often, entrepreneurs try to do too much for too many people and they dilute their efforts. The beachhead offer pulls out just one of those things and says, "This is the key frustration that I am trying to solve and here's how I'm doing it."

The beachhead analogy comes from the military world. Before you can make any headway into occupying enemy territory, you have to establish a foothold. Since the most effective way to deliver a lot of goods to a new territory is by ship, this foothold is often going to be on a beach.

In our context, the beach is the marketplace where other businesses are already solving problems. You have to land on something (your first, small solution), get a foothold, and make sure you can expand from there.

2. Test, fail, and iterate—but don't add too many options.
The second way out of Stage 1 is to experiment, fail fast and often, and iterate on the solutions you're putting out there. During this stage, the best thing you can do is the same thing you did when you were four years old. When children are young, they're sponges of information—just look at how quickly they pick up new languages. Children are learning new things about the world all the time, and as a businessperson you should be the same way.

You have to test whether the problem you're trying to solve is actually what the market wants to be solved. Sometimes you don't get that right, so you have to get your solution out there and see how the market responds to your language. See how people respond to the actual results of the solution you're providing, and then adapt. Stage 1 involves a lot of pivoting and changing things around.

What's critical here is that you don't add too many options to your beachhead offer because it's like running a science experiment where you want to control the number of factors that you are testing. If you have too many variables, it will be hard to see what's working and what's not.

Let's say you take your beachhead solution and try it in one particular market, and then you see that it doesn't work the way you thought it would. So you tweak that solution and try it again. Does it work? Does it get better results? Okay. You'll know one way or the other, and you can tweak that same solution again and again in that same market until you get it as right as it can be.

Compare that process to taking the solution to one market, seeing that it doesn't work, and then switching markets. In this situation, you don't know whether you had the right market with a slightly off solution or the wrong market with the right solution, or whether you had the right market with the right solution but didn't tell the story of your product—a.k.a. marketing—right. If you *happen* to have success in the second market, great; but if you don't, you're (usually) in a worse position than when you started.

To make this more concrete, let's say that you're coding a web application that solves a problem. You think that people will want certain features when solving that problem, so that's how you design the app. When you put it out there, it turns out those aren't the features people want. You're solving the frustration, but you're going to have to solve it another way. So you tweak your feature set until you come up with something that gets a good response from the market.

This process happens in service-based businesses, also. You think that one particular service methodology is the best way to solve certain problems, but it turns out that people want something else, so they don't respond to that original offer. So now you've got to change things. This refining process often occurs with books as well, as you're developing a manuscript out of workshop materials and speeches, and honing your ideas until you get the key messages that really resonate with your audience. The consistent positive feedback you're getting from a live audience is a good indication that you're on the right path.

Behind almost every successful solution is a lot of testing, failing, and iteration.

When you're in Stage 1 looking out at the people in Stage 4, you may be thinking, "They've got it all figured it out. Why aren't I there?" The answer is that they went through this learning and testing process; that's why they're there. And that's what your job is now—to test, fail, and iterate, while keeping your offers down to as few variables as possible.

As mentioned earlier, a chief challenge many Stage 1 entrepreneurs have is talking about what they do; keeping your offer simple makes talking about your solution easier. The more options you have, the more difficult it is to determine whether people are responding to feature X, Y, or Z. The more markets you approach at the same time, the trickier it is to get the feedback that you need to iterate in the right way.

3. Make sure your marketing revolves around or gets back to your beachhead solution.

People can be really scattered in Stage 1; there's a tendency to put a lot of different options and solutions into the marketplace. The more you focus your interactions with the marketplace around your beachhead offer, the more information you will get that will help you determine whether your offer is viable, whether you've homed in on your market's actual frustrations, and whether you're using the right language to get your message across to that market.

If your beachhead offer isn't getting attention, getting momentum is going to be very hard. Make sure that your marketing always comes back to that offer. That doesn't mean you're always trying to sell people your offer, but the themes you talk about need to be at least directing people that way so that you're establishing your brand in a way that reflects what you offer.

Be careful not to get into a situation where you're over-marketing and under-selling. There's a big difference between marketing and sales. Marketing activities are how you generate interest in and awareness of your product and brand. Sales activities are how you convert a prospect into a customer or client. Marketing is broadcasting a message to a group, while sales is about eliciting one particular action from one individual at a time.

Making it through Stage 1 requires you to:

1. Develop an offer that solves a frustration in the marketplace.

2. Sell that solution.

3. Assess whether your solution actually solves the problems and frustrations you've said it solves.

Without a clear, simple solution, you have nothing to sell. Without the right sales and marketing language, you won't have people to try out the solution. Without feedback from people who need your solution, you won't be able to tweak your offer until you get it right. And until you're actually solving the problem in the way people want it solved, you won't make any money. The way through Stage 1 is with a positive spiral of engagement with satisfied customers or clients.

The Catalytic Moment

In Stage 1, you'll over-buy, you'll over-invest, and you'll be distracted by every bright and shiny object that comes your way, and all of that is just part of the journey. The catalytic moment that moves you from Stage 1 to Stage 2 occurs when you have your first home run. Of all the different things you're trying, all the different seeds you're planting, one of them takes root and shoots up. You've managed to match a solution with a market and have found a compelling way to be a solution provider. This is where a lot of the fun starts. As you run the bases of that home run, you reach Stage 2.

Stage 1 Summary

- Stage 1 is the Entry stage. You have started the business, you're actively building your market and offers, and you're getting some traction. Congratulations—you're officially an entrepreneur.

- The challenges of Stage 1 are that you have to do a lot of small things and keep starting over; your marketing is not yet clear or targeted; and you have the pesky habit of undervaluing what you do.

- The strengths of Stage 1 are that you still have energy; you get the "success high" with every small win; and you're not too big to fail. Now is the time to fail fast and often and in relative obscurity.

- The inconvenient truth of Stage 1 is that you have no idea what you're doing.

- The ways ahead are to:

  1. Focus on your beachhead offer.

  2. Test, fail, and iterate—but don't add too many options (you need to control your variables).

  3. Make sure your marketing revolves around or gets back to your beachhead solution.

- The catalytic moment that takes you from Stage 1 to Stage 2 occurs when you have your first big success. You've matched a solution with a market and have found a compelling way to be a solution provider. Let the fun begin!

CHAPTER THREE
Stage 2: The Growth Stage

"The success combination in business is:
Do what you do better ... and: Do more of what you do...."
—David Joseph Schwartz

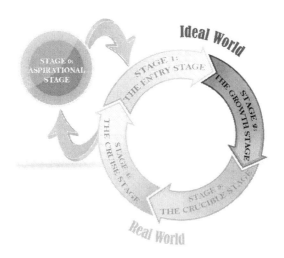

Stage 2 is the Growth stage. The business is already going, you have customers and market demand, you're feeling excited, and business is taking off. I like to refer to this stage as "riding the rocket." It's like you're holding onto this rocket, you're throwing in as much fuel as possible, and you're going faster and faster and faster—and that's fun. That's why this is the stage so many entrepreneurs and business builders love to stay in.

Challenges of Stage 2

The first challenge is that it's hard to ride a rocket. The faster the rocket goes, the tighter you have to hang onto it. The higher it goes, the harder it is to stay on. And, unfortunately, rockets aren't meant for long-term flying.

The second major challenge is that you have too many ideas. Because you've had a home run in one area, you start trying to replicate that all over the place. Ideas are streaming, your confidence is up, your excitement is up, and there is too much going on. A lot of Stage 2 entrepreneurs get overwhelmed and have a hard time figuring out what to do, because they simply have too many ideas. This is fundamentally different from Stage 3, when entrepreneurs have figured out how to manage having too many ideas but generally have too much work.

Another challenge is that you're not "there" yet. You're not quite playing with the big dogs yet, and they may not be paying any attention to you. You don't have the partnerships, audience, or tribe formed around what you do. You're having great success, but you're still just not quite there, and you kind of know it. You're saying things like "If only so-and-so would pay attention" or "If only such-and-such would happen, then I would be *there*." Wherever *there* is.

Strengths of Stage 2

Let's talk about the strengths of Stage 2. The biggest strength is that it's fun. It's fun to have an idea and to have it get picked up, accepted, and validated by the market. It's fun to have people interested in what you do. It's fun to be able to provide a solution for people who didn't have one; all of that is a blast. Again, it's why so many entrepreneurs want to stay in Stage 2.

The second strength is that there are a lot of possibilities. Your business still has a lot of room to grow, a lot of possible friendships and partnerships to make, and a lot of capacity for new things you can try because you're not at full capacity. Paradoxically, the faster your rocket goes, the fewer options you have because you can't turn it or stop it easily; Stage 2 is that sweet spot between going fast enough to have fun but not so fast and far that you find yourself on a fixed path.

Another strength is that you don't have those pseudo-entrepreneurial-existential crises about what you should be doing. You're in the moment, you're rocking it, and there's a feeling in Stage 2 that there's nothing on earth that you were meant to do other than this. Stage 2 is infectious.

The Inconvenient Truth

The inconvenient truth of Stage 2 is that you can't keep going like this. You can't continue to throw more and more fuel into the rocket and go faster and faster. At a certain point, you're going to fall off that rocket.

The Way Ahead

The way ahead is to start focusing on your market niche or specialty. In other words, start saying no to the many different possibilities and figure out what it is you're doing, with whom, and for what.

1. Add supporting or complementary offers.
A supporting solution is something like a workbook that supports the book you just sold. The solution might be a product,

an add-on to the application you developed, or an additional service beyond your core service. A complementary solution addresses a different but related frustration. The chief difference between the two types of offers is that a supporting solution cannot stand alone, whereas a complementary solution can be sold independently. The addition of supporting and complementary solutions presents huge opportunities for your business in Stage 2 and will make your journey through Stage 3 a lot easier.

For instance, let's take the problem of needing something to put a nail into two pieces of wood, assuming that there's a clear need for a nail as opposed to a screw, glue, or some other type of fastener. A common solution to that problem is a hammer. A supporting product might be the nail punch that allows you to drive the nail in under the surface of the wood. You can't use the nail punch without the hammer because you still have to hit the nail. A complementary product would be a pry bar that allows you to pull the nails out of the wood. The pry bar can be used independently of the hammer, but both tools are often needed for the same project.

To take the example further, different customers will have different needs for the same project. Much to my mixed adoration and frustration, my left-handed dad can effectively wield a hammer in his right hand while hitting a nail at an awkward angle, usually without being able to see the nail. Three hits, on target, and he's done. He needs a pry bar only when he's following my nailing jobs, and I know going into a nailing project that I'm going to need a pry bar. My dad passed on to me more of his urge to build stuff than his talent for doing so.

A healthy mix of supporting and complementary offers will allow you to best serve your market at the same time that it positively affects the average lifetime value of your customers. The higher the average lifetime value of your customers, the fewer customers you need in order to reach the same revenue numbers.

It's the natural evolution of establishing a beachhead to advance into the marketplace and grow outward; just be sure you're growing in a way that supports your beachhead solution and supports the brand you are trying to build.

Many entrepreneurs will take the opposite of the expand-from-your-beachhead approach and create what I call "terminal solutions." What makes a solution terminal is that there's no conceptual link between that solution and the others you offer. This is not to say that a link can't be made, but some links are harder to make than others. For example, let's say that you're selling "Eighteen Stretches to Heal Knee Pain" and then, because you see a market need somewhere, develop a product that easily removes grime from wheels. You *could* tie the two products together, but the reality is that a customer who buys your solution for knee pain is far less likely to buy your wheel-cleaning solution than to buy a solution that helps with hip pain.

When a customer purchases a terminal solution, there's no easy place for her to go from there without your providing a lot of additional marketing or education—two things, by the way, that many Stage 2 businesses are getting competent at. With few exceptions, what occurs more often is a wasted marketing and sales effort.

It's much easier to sell to satisfied customers because they know, like, and trust you. Terminal offers break this pattern because the customer often can't make the connection between your brand and its array of offers.

The example above might seem bizarre, but I have seen plenty of real businesses whose sets of offers are just as far apart or where one particular offering seems way out on its own in left field. Even when a terminal product does sell, it's hard to market because it doesn't resonate with your brand and you've essentially ended your customer relationship with that one sale. With complementary or supporting offers, on the other hand, you get that natural upward spiral of customer engagement in your business. You're continuing to solve their problems, and your brand makes sense to customers because all its offers are related.

2. Maintain your beachhead offer.

What I've seen happen so many times, and it's quite natural for this to happen, is that people will actually start getting traction on a beachhead solution. They're solving problems, people are loving the solution and loving the business for providing it, and then the businesses go and do something completely different.

While it's true that developing a different brand or business is similar to developing a terminal offer, the former is much worse. When people try to develop two major brands at the same time, they can't manage the growth and service that are required to maintain those two separate businesses and brands. The beachhead offer that they first established gets diluted and that business stops growing, while the second thing doesn't have the resources to really take off. Inevitably, one business gets put out to pasture, and in the meantime, all the resources it took to grow, maintain, and dismantle that business get pulled from the one that makes it, when instead all those resources could have been applied to the one growing business in the first place.

Unless whatever you're doing is truly dissonant with where you're trying to go, don't give up the ground that you've already established. Stay focused on your beachhead offer.

3. Keep riding the rocket and stay customer-facing and customer-focused.

This may sound counterintuitive, but you actually want to push your business to its limits so that you know, demonstrably, what real problems need to be fixed during Stage 3. If you slow down while you've got the momentum and initiative, it's easy to stagnate and stop growing altogether; momentum is one of those things in life and business that's hard to gain and easy to lose.

Because of the profuse positive attention they're receiving during this stage of business, many business owners feel the urge to slow down to make sure the business doesn't fall apart; for many of them—especially women, minorities, and creatives—it's the first time so much positive and public attention has been placed on them. That can be a lot to take, depending on where they are in their own personal journey. Additionally, we have a lot of limiting myths in our culture about the bad things that happen to people who are doing well and succeeding, so many people start anticipating a fall and try to prevent it.

At this point, many people will start to self-sabotage and pull back because the light on them is getting too bright and hot. Rather than propel ourselves forward, we tell ourselves the easy lie that we need to fix our business systems and work a few things out. (I'm a card-carrying member of this club, too.)

The idea of breaking your business is important because we entrepreneurs are capable of solving all sorts of problems. Yet many of the problems aren't *real* problems—they're things we made up. As Thomas Jefferson said, "How much pain they have cost us, the evils which have never happened."

If you wait until some of the things start breaking, you can solve the actual problems of your business rather than the fictional ones you come up with.

Until things start breaking, keep the rocket going, stay customer-facing, and try as best you can to stand in the light you're turning on.

The Catalytic Moment

The catalytic moment that moves you from Stage 2 to Stage 3 occurs when market demand exceeds your ability to deliver. Whatever you're doing is working, you can't do any more than you're currently doing, and there are so many opportunities available for your business that you don't have the systems, people, or processes in place to handle them long-term. When this happens, you move into the stage of business that almost every entrepreneur loathes.

Summary: Stage 2

- Stage 2 is the Growth stage. The business is already going, you have customers and market demand, you're feeling excited, and business is taking off. You're riding the rocket.

- The challenges of Stage 2 are that it's hard to ride a rocket; you have too many ideas; and you're not quite "there" yet.

- The strengths of Stage 2 are that it's fun; there are lots of possibilities; and you're in the zone.

- The inconvenient truth of Stage 2 is that you can't ride a rocket forever.

- The ways ahead are to:

  1. Add supporting or complementary offers (or both).

  2. Maintain your beachhead offer.

  3. Keep riding the rocket and stay customer-facing and customer-focused.

- The catalytic moment that takes you from Stage 2 to Stage 3 occurs when market demand exceeds your ability to deliver.

CHAPTER FOUR
Stage 3: The Crucible Stage

"The mark of a successful organization isn't whether or not it has problems; it's whether it has the same problems it had last year."
—John Foster Dulles

Stage 3 is the Crucible stage. This stage is awkward and challenging, as you bump against the edges of your business. There's a feeling of constriction and a sense that there's not enough ground under the business. Stage 3 is the first "no" stage. It's the time when you finally have to start practicing saying no because you're already at capacity.

If you've ever been in Stage 3, you know it. It's frustrating and disheartening. You spend time trying to figure out what small tweaks you have to make in order for your business to move forward. You've got enough going for you that it's hard to quit, but you don't have enough systems in place that you can continue to do this indefinitely. Seth Godin calls Stage 3 the "dip" stage of business.

Challenges of Stage 3

The first challenge of Stage 3 is that you're tired. You've been on the road for a while, you've been hanging onto the rocket, you've thrown as much fuel as you can into it, and you've taken the business about as far as you can on grit, spirit, and spunk.

The second challenge is that there's not really a business under the business. You're missing some or all of the administrative help, legal and tax implications, and everything else it takes to make a business tick.

The third challenge is that people are watching now. You're no longer in that safe stage where nobody is paying attention to you. Maybe the big dogs are starting to promote you and put you in front of their people. Now you have to be much more aware of the social game and the social expectations of your business. You're not that rogue business anymore; you're no longer the up-and-coming one.

Strengths of Stage 3

The first strength of Stage 3 is that you are a small giant. In whatever realm you're in, you are big enough to be a known player, but not so big that you're overextending or that people want to take you down. You can call upon a trusted group of friends or your network to get things done, you have some impact, and you have leverage to extend in this stage.

Another strength of Stage 3 is that you're at home as an entrepreneur. You've matured to the point of knowing that this is right for you. It has become part of your being in a way, so you no longer have to question it or spend a lot of energy explaining it. On a personal note, this is normally when your family and friends finally stop trying to convince you to do something else.

The last major strength is that you know what's working. You have your positioning, your marketing is clear enough to get sufficient sales, you've figured out the repeatable elements of your business that make it work, and you have a good idea of what's working and what's not.

The Inconvenient Truth

The inconvenient truth of Stage 3 is that there wasn't much business under the business. The growth of the business has largely depended on effort, intuition, fortuitous timing, and grit more than it has relied on a strategic sense of where the business is going, how it can get there, and who needs to be on the team to help it get there. To make it through Stage 3, you must get four key ingredients in place: the people, processes, systems, and positioning that drive your business.

The Way Ahead

The key principle to make it through Stage 3 is to focus on your core and shed the rest. This is the stage in which, by necessity, you have to look inward rather than outward because the chief challenges all have to do with your business's core people, systems, processes, and positioning. The three recommendations below highlight different ways to focus on your core.

Before we move there, though, it's important to acknowledge and celebrate that you're in Stage 3. As much as people hate being in Stage 3, the truth of it is that you have a lot to be proud of. Many businesses never actually make it here because they can't find a solution that matches the marketplace and they never develop a customer base. They never get a tribe. (Conversely, some businesses do reach Stage 3 but get stuck there because of the dynamic I call "founder's mojo"; for more on that, see the appendix.)

Fundamentally, having more demand for your offerings than you can serve is a great problem to have. Furthermore, the pains that you're feeling now are necessary in the same way that past romantic partners taught us how to appreciate and cherish the ones we're currently with. To echo Tennyson's "better to have loved and lost than never to have loved at all," it's better to have grown to your limits than never to have grown at all. With that perspective, let's dive right in.

1. Start working on your business's engine: reduce complexity, extraneous human effort, and information silos.

Businesses in Stage 3 of the small business life cycle have three major things going on:

1. There is a lot of complexity because problems, opportunities, and short-term fixes have been growing and popping up all over the place.

2. There's a lot of extraneous human effort.

3. There are many different information silos.

If you've built your business using the insights from this book, you're actually going to be well ahead of the game and things will make a lot more sense. There will still be some unneeded complexity and operational waste, but they'll be more limited.

To work on your business's engine, you'll want to reduce the complexity, any extraneous human effort, and the number of information silos. This stage is not fun for most people, and certainly not as much fun as solving other people's problems and getting those wins.

Additionally, working through your own stuff is much more challenging. If your business is in a mess, this means you have to recognize and own the impact that your behaviors, actions, and level of clarity have been having.

Taking the business you've built and breaking it down this way, piece by piece, can be tough, but it is the only way to stabilize the people, processes, systems, and positioning that make your business work.

Stage 3 is generally the first stage in which an entrepreneur must start thinking like a manager. That means either hiring a manager or becoming a manager. Now that you've defined your core business, it's time to enlist the management procedures or people needed to take care of that business for you, so that you can continue to drive the entire business forward.

Many small businesses are perennially stuck because they do not have enough hands on deck to maintain the business. They don't have enough execution power. There's a very obvious reason for this: usually, small businesses are bootstrapped from the beginning, meaning that there's not a lot of cash flow. As they grow, they eat through their cash. Nothing eats revenue like a growing company. That makes it hard to hire the people you need to come in and grow the business with you.

The creative visionaries who start businesses are often weak executors. They have big ideas. They have big strategies. They have big visions. And they may not want to do the actual work that's required to fulfill those plans, ideas, and visions.

When you're working on your business engine, you're looking at:

- Where are things too complex?
- Which extraneous human effort can be systematized?
- Where are the information silos?

Let's look more closely at information silos. An information silo is created when one person has information that's critical to the operations of the business but is not being shared with anyone else. One example we see all the time occurs when the CEO or the owner-executive is not sharing the annual plan with the people at the front line. So the people at the front line are largely operating on the context of where things are today, versus where this business is headed over the next couple of years.

Another common experience occurs when the sales staff has information that the service staff doesn't have and vice versa. The service staff knows that the business is at capacity, but the sales staff keeps selling anyway, or the service staff is concerned about a lull when the sales staff knows they're closing deals tomorrow.

Although some information silos are created because people are hoarding information and creating their own little fiefdoms, the more common culprit in small businesses is that people are overtaxed and don't have the processes and systems in place to support their sharing the information. The lack of these resources isn't their fault, and the burden to fix the problem shouldn't be placed on them; it's the responsibility of the executive team—even if the entire team is one person—to take the time to develop the resources.

If your team doesn't know where your business is going and where it is, chaos, diffusion, and confusion will be the key drivers of your business—and you inevitably won't want to go where they're taking it.

2. Review your revenue lines for margins, brand resonance, and sustainability.

By the time you reach Stage 3 in your business, it's prudent to start thinking in terms of margins versus absolute dollars. While it's fun to say that you have a six- or seven-figure business, that doesn't tell you how effectively you're operating.

Margins show you what percentage of every dollar you earn in revenue gets used before you can see any profit. For instance, a net margin of 35 percent means that for every dollar you earn, 65¢ of it goes to the business. A net margin of 50 percent means that the business eats only 50¢ of every dollar. Higher margins mean that you can earn less and keep the same amount; a business with a 33 percent net margin would have to earn around $303,000 in revenue for the owner to earn $100,000, whereas a business with a 50 percent margin would be able to do the same with $200,000. (This is a simplification of margins and earnings, for there are many variables and kinds of margins to consider, yet it illustrates the point. For a fuller explanation of margins, check out *Financial Intelligence*.)

When you look at a business in Stage 3, a lot of the extraneous human effort comes from selling things that are no longer profitable or as profitable as other things. As you're growing and scaling your business, you want to focus on those offers that have higher margins, because every dollar you make from those products and services puts more money either in your pocket or back into the business.

With many of my clients, after analyzing the full costs of running their businesses and selling their solutions, we could see that they were actually losing money by selling a certain product or service. When you look at marketing costs, delivery costs, production costs, payroll costs, taxes, and all the other things that may come out of that dollar that you make, it's easy to see how a business can be losing money for every sale it makes.

In Stage 3, when you're in a critical growth stage and there already aren't enough resources to go around, you definitely don't want to spend money on a big marketing campaign to push a product or service that's losing you money. Of course, you wouldn't want to do this at any stage, but losing money in Stage 3 is especially hard because you know what that money could be fueling if it were being used in other ways.

Each new solution that your business develops should be at least as profitable as the last solution you developed. The exception is if this new solution is primarily meant to acquire new customers whom you can sell a more profitable solution to down the road. Just be sure that you show customers of the old product the relationship between it and the new product, rather than leaving it up to them to find or make that link on their own.

Another factor to consider is brand resonance. Usually, the solution that you started with in Stage 1 is not the one you should stick with in the later stages. An astute reader might be thinking, "Okay, so you've been telling us the whole time to make sure that we maintain the ground we've established, that we should advance from our beachhead, and now you're telling us that maybe it was the wrong ground?"

No, I'm not telling you that. I'm telling you that the initial solution you came up with is generally a much smaller version of what you can create later on. So hanging onto that solution can impede the ability of your business to solve larger and more valuable problems for your customers or clients.

To evaluate your business's brand resonance, ask yourself, "Do our current products reflect our business accurately, or do they project a business that's less capable than our business is at meeting a wide and deep range of our market's needs? Are our solutions still relevant today for our market?"

That last question is especially important for products that serve the tech industry. The more your solutions depend upon changing technology, the more you'll have to make sure that your products are still relevant.

A last consideration when you're looking at your revenue lines is sustainability. When we talk about sustainability in small business, we're not necessarily talking about sustainability for the environment or the planet. We're talking about whether the business can maintain what it's doing in perpetuity. To determine this, you need to address the following three considerations.

First, can the people on the team continue to serve this product? Are they still having fun? Is there still passion? Is there still a sense of service? Without those, your business will atrophy and you'll lose your key players.

Second, is the business making enough money to continue? This is what reviewing and understanding your margins helps with. If you're losing money with some or all of your offers, that's not sustainable. This endeavor may just be a really expensive hobby that you like dumping money into, but most of us are not in business to lose money.

Third, will your business be able to keep up with the changing needs of customers in the future? Markets change. New technological options change what we want and they change our frustrations.

Take pay phones, for instance. Maintaining them used to be a big business, but with the introduction of cell phones, pay phones quickly became obsolete, so all the companies that supported the pay phone industry found themselves with a problem: they could no longer be viable in the new world where cell phones existed.

You have to carefully consider whether your business will be able to take care of your current customers now, whether you'll be able to take care of those customers three years from now, and whether you'll still be able to acquire new customers three years from now.

3. Mine the gold in your back-end pipeline.

Sometimes people resist the systemization and fine-tuning of their businesses because they want to continue to generate new customers. There's a fear that if they change what's been working, they'll lose revenue.

That fear is understandable, but turns out to be dead wrong.

As businesses grow, there's always a group of customers who become fans and champions of your brand. These fans and champions are in what I call the "back-end sales pipeline," as opposed to the "front-end sales pipeline" that so many marketers and salespeople want to focus on. Your back-end sales pipeline is filled with satisfied customers and clients who, more often than not, are being forgotten about.

Many people in Stage 3 tend to look out into the marketplace for opportunities to generate new customers, and they're completely overlooking the fact that they have a list of people who are a phone call, an email, or a marketing pitch away from buying something today. I commented earlier that it's easier to sell something new to a satisfied customer than it is to create a new customer. Stage 3 businesses tend to have a large list of previous customers, yet they're not engaging with them by following up, checking to see how the solution is working, or offering them anything new.

Now is the time when you can recoup all of those marketing resources you spent in acquiring your current customers, because with a much smaller effort you can earn the same amount of money by engaging the people in your back-end pipeline. That frees you up to focus on growing and developing your business engine.

You don't have to choose between systemizing your business and generating revenue. You can work on getting the business right and still make more money by focusing on existing customers, rather than trying to pull in new customers whom you might not be able to serve as well.

The Catalytic Moment

The catalytic moment of Stage 3 occurs when your business backbone gels. **You get your people, processes, systems, and positioning in place.** Whatever your business does, how it does it, and whomever it does it with, this can now happen efficiently, effectively, and indefinitely.

Here's something else about Stage 3: when you're in Stage 3, there's a lot of disequilibrium and seesawing back and forth between Stage 2 and Stage 4. Largely, that's because when you get one piece of the puzzle in place, another one pops out.

For instance, you might get your revenue up, but neglect to anticipate the tax implications of the new revenue. Or maybe, out of exasperation, you try something new and it works, so you chase that down and it puts you in Stage 2, but you eventually get back to the same problem you tried to avoid in the first place. People in Stage 3 often see this process as circular, but it's actually more like a corkscrew.

The life of business is such that there will always be changes, seesaws, and ups and downs. Once you reach Stage 4, though, the turbulence doesn't break anything or cause major setbacks. You know what's going on and how to fix it—or whether it's something that doesn't require fixing because it's something you can wait out.

Once you reach this point of perspective, control, and security, you've reached Stage 4.

Stage 3 Summary

- Stage 3 is the Crucible stage. You're at the delightfully frustrating point at which you're booked solid and working at full steam, but the demand for your goods and services outstrips your ability to meet it. Something has to give.

- The challenges of Stage 3 are that you're tired; the business is resting on shaky supports and is missing some systems; and people are watching now. Goodbye, anonymity.

- The strengths of Stage 3 are that you're a small giant; you're at home as an entrepreneur; and you know what's working.

- The inconvenient truth of Stage 3 is that there isn't much business under the business. You need structure, systems, teams, processes, and other fun stuff like that.

- The ways ahead are to:

  1. Start working on your business's engine: reduce complexity, extraneous human effort, and information silos.

  2. Review your revenue lines for margins, brand resonance, and sustainability.

  3. Mine the gold in your back-end pipeline.

- The catalytic moment that takes you from Stage 3 to Stage 4 occurs when your business backbone gels. You get your systems, processes, people, and positioning in place.

CHAPTER FIVE
Stage 4: The Cruise Stage

"Keep your eyes on the stars, and your feet on the ground."
—Theodore Roosevelt

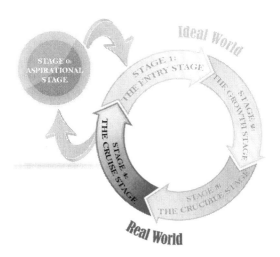

Finally, Stage 4 is the lauded Cruise stage. You've got your people, processes, systems, and positioning in place. You focus on the things you can do indefinitely that meet that sweet spot between market demand, your interest, and what you can do long-term. A business in Stage 4 is like a supersonic jet; it can move incredibly fast, but it has to turn slowly or else it'll be torn apart.

Challenges of Stage 4

The first challenge of Stage 4 is that you switch from riding the rocket to playing the long, patient game. You've reached a level of business expertise and positioning where the only way you're going to get better is to focus on the long game of increasing expertise and market share.

Another challenge is that you have a lot to lose to a competitor or another mishap. There are relationships you've spent years building, with the resulting social trust. There is your profitability and the ability to hire teammates and keep them thriving with you. There's so much at stake in Stage 4 that it becomes too much for some entrepreneurs to bear, especially those who started a business to do whatever it was they were doing. If they started a pie shop, it was so they could bake pies, not so they could franchise pie shops or manage other people baking pies.

Perhaps the biggest challenge of Stage 4 is Bright Shiny Object Syndrome. At Stage 4, trying new things, doing a lot, and dramatically changing your business structure can send your supersonic jet crashing to the ground. However, the hyper-creative innovator part of us always wants to build something, and we're lured by new potentials.

Generally, this temptation is what moves us from Stage 4 to an earlier stage. We do something crazy like write a book, form a new partnership, go public, or introduce offers to a new market. There are all sorts of things we can do that push us back down. Sometimes, though, what happens to get us out of Stage 4 is completely unanticipated; maybe there's a death in the family or another dramatic life event, like a divorce, or maybe a key team member is hired away. What's important about the volatility in

Stage 4 is that it's almost all internal because by now you've mastered the external conditions that would otherwise threaten your business.

Strengths of Stage 4

In the Cruise stage, the first main strength is that your business is a well-oiled machine. You've got your people, processes, systems, and positioning in place. As much as entrepreneurs hate to say and hear "That's the way we do things around here," there are few things better for a small business than for the entire team to know exactly how the team operates.

Another strength of Stage 4 is that you have leverage. You're a known player, you're a powerful player, and you have the resources to be able to extend in different ways. When your business needs more money, your team knows how to solve that problem. If your business needs more capacity, your team knows how to solve that problem, too. You know how to fix any external problem that comes up. (It's the internal problems, like the temptation of bright shiny objects, that are hard for any small business owner to temper.)

The last strength, and this one's really important and not talked about a lot, is that money and profit largely become secondary to the mission of your business. With enough success and sustainable command across the board, you've reached what I like to call your "sufficiency number" and you're no longer motivated primarily by the money.

Now your business gets to do some risky and remarkable things because it doesn't have to solve the basic problems of a growing business. When money becomes secondary, you can truly focus on your mission and the legacy of your business. Read *Good to Great* or *It's Not About the Coffee* for more about how businesses move past the basic profitable stage or about executives who are focused on doing truly remarkable things.

The Inconvenient Truth

The inconvenient truth of Stage 4 is that you can move fast but you can't turn quickly. That's what makes this another "no" stage. In Stages 1 and 2, you can do a lot of swerving back and forth. The scale and scope of your business are such that you can still pivot. At Stage 4, by the time you get those people, processes, systems, and positioning in place, you can't do much turning. You can't do something different without creating confusion for the people and businesses around you.

As the person who's been part of the business from its earliest stages all the way to its end stages, you might feel as if you're not going anywhere, even though you're moving really fast. That can be frustrating.

The Way Ahead

Now that you're at the end of the business life cycle, you might be wondering where you should be looking. Stage 4 was where you were trying to get to, right? Remember that this is a cycle, and it's possible to move into earlier stages at almost any time.

You have so many resources available to you at this point. Your business becomes very dynamic because now you can choose to do just about anything you want to do. It's possible to take your business in a completely different direction and break the success you've had. It's also possible to take it in a slightly different direction and maintain the success you've had.

1. Scale (intelligently).

To make it through Stage 4, you'll need to focus on three main tasks. The first is to scale intelligently. Stage 4 is the stage in which you can scale your business indefinitely because you have your people, your processes, your systems, and your positioning in place. You know how to hire new people, you know what those new people need to do, you know how to get new customers, and you know what those customers want. You know so much that you did not know in Stage 1—it is a wonderful place to be.

However, scaling a business five times or ten times is not as easy as you would think, and it's important to consider whether or not you want to scale your business. It is perfectly acceptable to reach a level of steady growth and decide not to grow past that. You don't have to be Walmart, you don't have to be Apple, and you don't have to be Amazon.com. You can be that killer local business that takes care of its team, community, and owners.

As you start thinking about scaling, look at the real motivations behind it. I have a bias here that the real motivation behind scaling should be serving your customers and community, but you don't have to accept that. Can you scale the business profitably, while focusing on aligned growth that continues to serve you, your team, and your community?

By the time you start scaling 5x or 10x, you're going to need new managers and advisors, and you'll need to find different sources of funding. Your business is going to change dramatically. For instance, changing your business from a local model or a one-business model to a franchise model is actually like starting your business along Stage 1 of a new business life cycle. What it takes to manage a franchise operation is a lot different from what it takes to manage a single business unit. Likewise, taking on angel investors would also bring you into a new stage in a different life cycle of business.

When you radically change the dynamics of your business, you end up along a different phase of the journey. You can use a lot of what you've learned, but you also have to unlearn a lot of things in order to be successful in that new life cycle.

2. Make your key players as obsolete as possible.

This is another principle that might sound counterintuitive, but at this stage, you want to make your key players as obsolete as possible, meaning that the business can run without them. Doing this supports scaling, but it also supports your living the type of life you want to live. Many successful owner-executives get to Stage 4, but they have never figured out how to make themselves obsolete. The systems, processes, and positioning must support this gradual displacement of the owner-executive.

Interchangeability of key players is crucial in Stage 4 for there to be any sense of real security. As the owner-executive ages, as people get sick or move on, as your key players experience various life changes, you need to have training protocols in place, and systems and processes need to be documented.

What if a key player gets out of alignment with the rest of the team and decides to start a new business? If that key player was your chief salesperson, he's likely going to take those sales and relationships with him. Even if his contract has a non-compete clause, some things will legally fall outside of that.

If you haven't made key players obsolete, you're in this supersonic jet that is very brittle; one thing changes, and all of a sudden it doesn't work the same way. Then you go back into Stage 3 or even Stage 1 as you try to figure out how to run the business without that key player.

3. Develop a BSO warning indicator: look out for the words "new," "fun," "cool," and "easy."

BSO stands for "bright shiny object." Bright shiny objects are the bane of many a business because the owner, executives, CEO, and key players latch onto something new that alters the business's ability to operate.

It turns out that there are four words you can use as BSO warning indicators: new, fun, cool, and easy. If you've got two of them together, it's an even clearer sign that whatever this opportunity is, your interest in the solution is more about your personal levels of boredom or excitement than about where your market is.

Once you get that BSO warning indicator, you want to ask this series of questions:

- Where does this opportunity fit into our current business?
- How will this new thing affect our current operations?
- Does it change our plans, and what will we need to shift around to make it work?
- How does this new thing serve our audience better or differently than our current solutions?

If you're going to try something new, you want to go in with eyes wide open. As we discussed in Stage 3, any new offer should be at least as profitable as your existing solutions, or it should be able to generate customers to whom you can later sell higher-profit items.

A lot of BSOs do not meet either criterion—they reflect the current emotional state of the key players of the business more than they reflect any true need of the business or the marketplace.

I want to be very clear here: I'm not saying that you do not get to have fun in Stage 4. There are plenty of new things you can do that will be fun but will not alter your business's operations, your brand, or the way your market understands you. What I am saying is, just because it's fun doesn't mean you should do it.

When you're considering chasing after a BSO, be sure to remember what Stages 1 and 3 felt like, because a BSO is going to take you back to one of those two places. Either you'll be back in the Entry stage all over again, or you'll be heading back into Stage 3 as you unintentionally break the alignment of the people, processes, systems, or positioning that got you where you are now.

If you're looking for fun, consider going on a vacation instead of starting a new business. Don't risk the success that you have generated so far.

Stage 4 is a wonderful place to be, and the joy that you get out of a Stage 4 business is different from what you get out of a Stage 2 business. Both are a lot of fun, but when you're in a Stage 4 business, you know it's going to be there for you year after year. It's going to continue to grow so that it takes care of you, your team, and your community.

The Catalytic Moment

The catalytic moment that moves you from Stage 4 to lower stages of business occurs when you introduce a new brand or business dynamic. If you find that you need to create something new, I've got a very easy recipe for you: Go back and read what you need to do in Stage 0.

Summary: Stage 4

- Stage 4 is the Cruise stage. You've figured out what it was that kept you bottlenecked and constricted at Stage 3, you've fixed it, and you're running full steam ahead.

- The challenges of Stage 4 are that you need to switch from riding the rocket to playing the long game; you have a lot to lose; and you might get distracted by Bright Shiny Object Syndrome.

- The strengths of Stage 4 are that your business is a well-oiled machine; you have leverage; and money and profit become secondary to the mission of your business.

- The inconvenient truth of Stage 4 is that you can move fast but you can't turn quickly. You can't do something different without creating confusion for the people and businesses around you.

- The ways ahead are to:
    1. Scale intelligently.
    2. Make your key players as obsolete as possible.
    3. Develop a BSO warning indicator: look out for the words "new," "fun," "cool," and "easy."
- The catalytic moment that moves you from Stage 4 to lower stages occurs when you introduce a new brand or business dynamic. If you reeeeally need to create something new, go back and read the chapter on Stage 0.

CLOSING THOUGHTS

Remember that business is a life cycle. You can vacillate between a couple of stages for a while before you move on from them. With this guide, I wanted to show you what to watch out for, so you can make better strategic choices about how to work your way through business.

You know that if you're in Stage 1, it's going to be awkward and you're not going to know everything that you need to do, but now you also know how to keep moving forward in the face of uncertainty and perhaps unfavorable market conditions.

Conversely, if you're in Stage 4, you know that Bright Shiny Object Syndrome is going to pop up. It's not that you can't say yes to things; it's that you need to say yes slowly and intelligently, making sure that the new things fit either your business's strategy or your personal strategy. You don't want to throw everything off just because Apple introduced a new gadget that you want to use.

The world of small business and microbusiness is very challenging. More and more businesses are entering this realm because technology, social expectations, and the demands of life favor small businesses. Yet that means there will be more competition. Small business owners need to know more in order to be successful in this landscape.

Whatever stage of this journey you're in, that's okay. You know what you need to do to move forward, and you know that you're not alone. **Thank you for being in business.**

A RECAP OF THE
SMALL BUSINESS LIFE CYCLE

Stage 0

- Stage 0 is the Aspirational stage. You're thinking about starting a business or new venture but haven't yet done so.

- The challenges of Stage 0 are that choosing a business can be hard because there are so many possibilities; it's hard to make the leap from having a conventional job to being an entrepreneur; and the idea of changing the world can seem overwhelming.

- The strengths of Stage 0 are that you still have hope; you have a lot of energy; and anything counts as a win.

- The inconvenient truth of Stage 0 is that your idea might not work.

- The ways ahead are to:

    1. Start noticing what makes you come alive, along with what types of things you're natively good at and which kinds of people fire you up.

    2. Look for frustrations you can solve.

    3. Pick one frustration and start generating solutions.

- The catalytic moment that takes you from Stage 0 to Stage 1 occurs when something you try, works; you start to believe that you can do this; and you start that business.

Stage 1

- Stage 1 is the Entry stage. You have started the business, you're actively building your market and offers, and you're getting some traction. Congratulations—you're officially an entrepreneur.

- The challenges of Stage 1 are that you have to do a lot of small things and keep starting over; your marketing is not yet clear or targeted; and you have the pesky habit of undervaluing what you do.

- The strengths of Stage 1 are that you still have energy; you get the "success high" with every small win; and you're not too big to fail. Now is the time to fail fast and often and in relative obscurity.

- The inconvenient truth of Stage 1 is that you have no idea what you're doing.

- The ways ahead are to:

  1. Focus on your beachhead offer.

  2. Test, fail, and iterate—but don't add too many options (you need to control your variables).

  3. Make sure your marketing revolves around or gets back to your beachhead solution.

- The catalytic moment that takes you from Stage 1 to Stage 2 occurs when you have your first big success. You've matched a solution with a market and have found a compelling way to be a solution provider. Let the fun begin!

Stage 2

- Stage 2 is the Growth stage. The business is already going, you have customers and market demand, you're feeling excited, and business is taking off. You're riding the rocket.

- The challenges of Stage 2 are that it's hard to ride a rocket; you have too many ideas; and you're not quite "there" yet.

- The strengths of Stage 2 are that it's fun; there are lots of possibilities; and you're in the zone.

- The inconvenient truth of Stage 2 is that you can't ride a rocket forever.

- The ways ahead are to:

  1. Add supporting or complementary offers (or both).

  2. Maintain your beachhead offer.

  3. Keep riding the rocket and stay customer-facing and customer-focused.

- The catalytic moment that takes you from Stage 2 to Stage 3 occurs when market demand exceeds your ability to deliver.

Stage 3

- Stage 3 is the Crucible stage. You're at the delightfully frustrating point at which you're booked solid and working at full steam, but the demand for your goods and services outstrips your ability to meet it. Something has to give.

- The challenges of Stage 3 are that you're tired; the business is resting on shaky supports and is missing some systems; and people are watching now. Goodbye, anonymity.

- The strengths of Stage 3 are that you're a small giant; you're at home as an entrepreneur; and you know what's working.

- The inconvenient truth of Stage 3 is that there isn't much business under the business. You need structure, systems, teams, processes, and other fun stuff like that.

- The ways ahead are to:

    1. Start working on your business's engine: reduce complexity, extraneous human effort, and information silos.

    2. Review your revenue lines for margins, brand resonance, and sustainability.

    3. Mine the gold in your back-end pipeline.

- The catalytic moment that takes you from Stage 3 to Stage 4 occurs when your business backbone gels. You get your systems, processes, people, and positioning in place.

Stage 4

- Stage 4 is the Cruise stage. You've figured out what it was that kept you bottlenecked and constricted at Stage 3, you've fixed it, and you're running full steam ahead.

- The challenges of Stage 4 are that you need to switch from riding the rocket to playing the long game; you have a lot to lose; and you might get distracted by Bright Shiny Object Syndrome.

- The strengths of Stage 4 are that your business is a well-oiled machine; you have leverage; and money and profit become secondary to the mission of your business.

- The inconvenient truth of Stage 4 is that you can move fast but you can't turn quickly. You can't do something different without creating confusion for the people and businesses around you.

- The ways ahead are to:

  1. Scale intelligently.

  2. Make your key players as obsolete as possible.

  3. Develop a BSO warning indicator: look out for the words "new," "fun," "cool," and "easy."

- The catalytic moment that moves you from Stage 4 to lower stages occurs when you introduce a new brand or business dynamic. If you reeeeally need to create something new, go back and read the chapter on Stage 0.

APPENDIX
Understanding Founder's Mojo

Working with hundreds of small business owners has gotten me used to noticing and addressing patterns that apply across businesses. One ubiquitous dynamic I've seen in my fieldwork involves what I'm calling founder's mojo, which can be used to exponentially grow a business but can also prevent a business from growing.

Founder's mojo is that amalgam of intuition, vision, experience, and drivenness that enables a founder to be more effective, decisive, and risk-tolerant than the rest of her team. In the past, I've called this combination of traits the E-factor, but the E-factor and founder's mojo amount to the same thing.

Founder's mojo is what powers the creation and growth of early-stage businesses. It's also what keeps them stuck in Stage 3.

Founder's mojo is like an electric generator that can move around in a business. That generator can power *anything* within the business; in fact, it *has* powered everything in the business.

But there are only so many things the generator can power at once. As a business grows, there are more things needing juice than the generator can power simultaneously. When businesses are newer, it's possible to run around plugging in a few things that need juice, but as businesses grow, the running around starts to take considerably more energy. Many founders find themselves exhausted from it and feel frustrated because they never really charge anything up—they just keep things running.

And therein lies the rub with founder's mojo: it powers only what it's directly connected to. *No founder, no energy, no activity.* Business is not a frictionless plane, and without the infusion of more energy, things will slow down and eventually stop. Alas that the business ball seems to roll down the hill more readily and quickly than it rolls itself uphill.

"No founder" here doesn't necessarily refer to death; rather, it refers to the founder's not being plugged into a given activity. Most small business owners resist taking vacations or breaks because they know or believe that their business moves forward only when they're around to power it.

The reality of founder's mojo makes it such that there are only a few options in a small business:

1. Keep the business small enough that founder's mojo can power everything it needs to. (This is the route of micro-businesses, although most successful ones apply a lot of automation or software-driven processes.)

2. Continually fight with the frustration that comes from the consequences of having a business powered by one person—it runs only as fast and as well as you do.

3. Get the right people, processes, and systems in place—we're looking at right-sizing here, not growth for growth's sake.

Let's assume that no one wants to live in that second option.

It turns out that being successful with options 1 and 3 require a deeper look into the founder's most important job.

The Founder's Most Important Job

The upshot of understanding founder's mojo is that you can use it more effectively. Imagine it this way: with one unit of founder's mojo, either you can do the things that yield one unit of return, or you can do the things that yield ten units of return. Your limited energy should go to the latter option every time.

I've come to understand that the most important job of founders, leaders, and executives is to create order out of chaos.

This executive-level process of creating order out of chaos lies not in organizing books and papers, but rather in organizing people, activity, and resources. The very act of creating a business is an illuminating case of this principle: a successful startup taps into the existing flux of needs, desires, aspirations, challenges, and money and creates solutions that channel those energies to get people what they want and need. Startups that try to *create* too many of those factors struggle for a long time— they're digging holes rather than filling the ones already there.

"Chaos," for many people, has become an emotive word, as if there needs to be an exclamation or some negative emoticon that rides along with it. My meaning is closer to "disorder" and it's not necessarily negative; we need chaos as much as we need order to have thriving businesses, for chaos generates creative tension that later leads to insight and innovation.

The growth opportunities for most businesses lie in two places: at the core of the business and at its edges. We focus on growth at the core when we grapple with the toughest challenges of the business and work on our business systems. We focus on growth at the edges when we explore new solutions to create, find ways to reframe our current solutions for new markets, or create disruptive ripples that generate positive changes and opportunities for our business. Chaos is normally the greatest at the core and edges of a business.

Between those edges, though, is a vast number of things that do not require founder's mojo. A manager's job, for instance, is to maintain and make iterative improvements on the order that someone else has given him. Bookkeeping, though an essential part of business, is not something that requires founder's mojo; evaluating the financial performance of the company and making constructive changes *do*.

If the founder isn't placing some mojo on those tough challenges and edge-growth opportunities, no one else is. Employees can't, simply because they don't have founder's mojo. When a founder, executive, or leader tries to delegate the responsibility to jump in there, the result is BOPSAT—a Bunch of People Sitting Around Talking. BOPSAT rarely leads to effective change, and yes, it happens in small businesses just as frequently as it happens in larger organizations. Ultimately, the founder needs to get involved, make a decision, express priorities, and get people moving.

As part of the process, though, the founder needs to be sharing how those decisions are made so that people don't have to make the same kinds of decisions over and over. This sharing is one of those "growth at the core" activities. Many small businesses get stuck in Stage 3 precisely because their founders haven't shared their decision-making process; they've been the founders-managers-doers for so long that they're not seeing the three different hats they're wearing and not seeing that, at some point, other people need to be wearing two of those hats.

Five Ways Founders Stifle Business Growth

So why do founders keep all those hats on, even when they don't want to?

Past a certain stage of business, it's impossible for founders to effectively stay on top of all of the important functions in the four key dimensions of business—strategy, marketing, operations, and finance. What tends to happen is that they get stuck in operations—to use Michael Gerber's phrase on this one, they're working *in* the business, not *on* the business. Since all of their founder's mojo is consumed either by what they're working on in operations or by the switching costs of jumping from thing to thing, there's not much mojo left to tend to the other dimensions of business.

So, at precisely the time when founders should asking the five critical strategic questions about their business, they're usually doing something else instead. In the worst cases, they're working on yesterday's business, and in the best cases, they're asking those critical questions but haven't yet put the right processes, systems, and people in place to help them address the answers to the questions.

To build a thriving, sustainable company, founders have to move from being the chief firefighter to being the chief future-builder.

Most founders know where they need to go and know that they're stuck in the firefighting loop. Sometimes they don't know *why* they're stuck there, though, so the discussion that follows talks about the most common pattern I've observed.

#1: The bootstrapper mindset

Initiative and vision are two hallmark characteristics of bootstrappers. They're the kind of people who see that something needs to be done and don't wait around for someone else to do it.

This "I'm doing it because it needs to get done" mindset is absolutely essential for starting businesses. This mindset and a tolerance for uncertainty are what separate the people who start businesses from the people who've been thinking about starting a business for decades. (It's also the difference-maker between people who get promoted and people who hit a ceiling—while there is definitely a floor for bootstrappers, there is no ceiling.) Over time, though, the healthy bootstrapper mindset turns into …

#2: The bootstrapper habit

Eventually, bootstrappers stop thinking about what they're getting involved in because the mindset has turned into a stimulus-response habit. If something shows up on their action list, they start taking action.

As they continually take those actions, they build an efficiency curve with what they're doing. If initiative and vision are the seeds of founder's mojo, the founder's familiarity with and repetition of the foundational activities of the business are the water that makes it grow.

The downside to this efficiency curve, though, is that even when they start seeing that there's more to be done than they can do, founders don't start hiring and delegating, because their teammates are just so much slower than the founders, even after they've trained those teammates. Why spend all that time hiring someone and training someone only to have that person be a third as fast as you? (I get this one all the time.)

Let's just sidestep the fact that founders usually start businesses in a field in which they've already logged many of their ten thousand hours **and** someone else probably trained them **and** they've accrued more of those hours in the context of their own business. It's impossible for someone else to come in and perform at the level of the founder unless the founder hires someone who's doing something the founder doesn't know how to do.

Bootstrappers see the world a certain way and forget that other people don't see the world that way, too. They're often rather frustrated to find that the people they hire need to be told what to do and, in the earlier stages of their employment, how to do it.

Bootstrappers believe that people should just get hired and start doing what needs to be done because that's exactly what the bootstrappers would do.

Many founders dabble in hiring and find themselves quite disappointed. From their point of view, the people they hire are slow and lacking initiative. Founders therefore hire people only when it's absolutely necessary and for the minimal amount of time required for their teammates to do what they need to do.

Which leads to…

#3: Having to sort through the bucket of marbles
Let's imagine that founders' core tasks are a certain kind of marble in a bucket of myriad kinds of marbles. Founders need to see, process, and work with only one kind of marble in the bucket.

To get to those marbles, they have to dig around in all the other kinds of marbles. But since they have the bootstrapper habit, they see, process, and work on all the marbles. They're already there, after all—why not just go ahead and get it taken care of?

Even if they *don't* work on the other marbles, either they have to inhibit their natural impulse—and inhibition is the most taxing of the cognitive functions—or they have to wonder who's going to mess with all of the marbles and when they're going to do it. And if they're paying people, why are there so many damn marbles in the bucket in the first place?

These bootstrappers have yet to train their teammates to hand them the marbles they need to see or train themselves to focus only on their own marbles. The primary reason they haven't trained their teammates boils down to…

#4: Insufficient trust
Although insufficient trust is #4 on the list, it's really the root cause of why so many businesses get stuck. Founders strangle the growth of their companies because they just won't let go—they

become behavioral control freaks even if they don't view themselves as such or even despise control freaks.

If founders don't understand founder's mojo, it's easy for them to distrust their teammates' ability to perform well. Most of their experience is with people who aren't as efficient and proactive as they are, because even if those people see what needs to be done, they don't know how to do it. They'd either have to spend a lot of time figuring it out or pay someone else to, which amounts to the same thing—lost revenue. So, revenue is lost because the founder could be going out and getting more customers or funding, or because she has to pay someone else. Is all the effort of hiring, training, and supervising other people to do something the founder can do better really worth it?

Underneath all of this questioning of teammates' actual or potential performance is that founders don't trust themselves. Did they build a business that will make it? Did they pick the right strategy, business model, and market? Are they actually going to be able to lead and pay people month to month? What if it doesn't work?

Inside the armor of confidence, resilience, gumption, and brilliance that founders don to get things done is a squishy human being who's battling shades of the demons we all face.

#5: The value crisis
"If I'm not involved in the day-to-day operations of the business, what will I do? What am I contributing to the business?"

I've heard these questions or variants of them quite a few times, too, and I've learned to prepare my clients for them as their businesses get close to Stage 4. The founders' day-to-day experience slows down substantially because the people they've hired and the systems they've created are rapidly replacing them. Because most early-stage businesses are built via the Fred Flintstone method—for the business to grow faster, the founder's feet have to move faster—the founders' operating assumptions tell them that their moving slowly means that the business is moving slowly.

Once these founders slow down, they can start to think about things at a deeper level than they have before. They become aware that the kind of leadership that's required at the current stage of business is much different from what they've been delivering as a leader up to this point. They have to learn to work *through people*—which means trusting more, leading more, and letting people do their jobs without interfering with them, even if the way someone's team goes about doing their jobs is different from the way the founder would or did do it.

Long-term considerations like compensation planning, benefits improvements, and succession planning become more important, because the question founders must answer now is not "how do I solve today's challenges or pursue today's opportunities?" but rather "how do I ensure that other people can solve tomorrow's challenges and know which opportunities to pursue?" Founders have to figure out either how to retain the people on the team for the long haul or how to teach those people to hire, train, and mentor the people who will be on the team in the coming years.

And, lastly, some founders will start to take their exit plan seriously because they recognize that, finally, the business can survive and perhaps thrive without their founder's mojo. They recognize that their true value is not their personal value, but the value of the enduring company they've created.

Founder's Mojo + Trust = Long-Term Success

While this particular discussion has highlighted how founder's mojo stifles business growth, it's important that we remember two things: it's the way that mojo is being used that can put a stranglehold on the business; and the founder's insight, attention, and willpower are crucial ingredients of the business's secret sauce. Founders should not power down their mojo, but they should make sure they're using it to work on the growth points of the business.

Trusting their strategy, their team, and their systems enables founders to use their mojo constructively because it allows them to turn the reins over to other people who can drive the business while the founders steer the business in the right direction. With a well-defined strategy, smart, committed people can figure out how to get where founders want to go, but only if those founders are providing sufficient leadership.

While I've seen this time and time again in the world of business, I learned this lesson as a military officer. If you take care of your people and do your job as a commander, everything else works out. You don't have to be everywhere—you can't be everywhere, anyway—but good leaders don't have to be physically present for their presence to be felt. Providing leadership and building trust are how generals command legions and captains command companies.

And it turns out that providing leadership and building trust are also how great founders build enduring, remarkable companies.

SUGGESTIONS FOR FURTHER READING

Rather than attempting to provide an exhaustive list of books, I'm providing a shorter list so that you can quickly decide which book to jump into. You'll notice that they either highlight the specific challenges small business owners face or discuss important insights about business growth and management.

Innovation and Entrepreneurship by Peter Drucker

This is a classic for good reason. It discusses the sources of innovation and the practice of entrepreneurial management. It's not the easiest read, but it's well worth the effort.

Crossing the Chasm by Geoffrey Moore

This book discusses the stages in which new solutions and products are adopted by the marketplace. Knowing where your business's solutions are in the adoption curve allows you to market them appropriately. Don't let its tech bias fool you; many products and services seem new to many markets, even though they've been around for a while.

Good to Great by Jim Collins

This influential book examines what great businesses do to excel. It was the first book to introduce the Hedgehog Concept (the importance of understanding the intersection between what you're deeply passionate about, what you can be the best in the world at, and what drives your economic engine), as well as many other key insights about business success.

Purple Cow by Seth Godin

Your business has to stand out to be successful. This best-selling book discusses how to move from a me-too business to one that's truly remarkable.

Fierce Conversations by Susan Scott

Many people don't know how to have honest, constructive, and uncomfortable conversations with the people around them, and one of the challenges of small business is that your coworkers aren't just nameless faces—they're your friends, family, and people you care deeply about. This book shows you how to have catalytic conversations, rather than either avoiding the hard stuff or exploding when hard stuff comes up.

The Personal MBA by Josh Kaufman

Whether you went to school for an MBA or ended up with an experiential one, this book is a great refresher course on the key insights, frameworks, and tools required to be a successful small business executive.

Financial Intelligence by Karen Berman and Joe Knight

What's a net profit margin, and why should you care? What does your balance sheet tell you? What's the difference between profit and cash? This book helps you figure out what the numbers mean and how to use them to make business decisions.

Predictably Irrational by Dan Ariely

Many economists posit a rational buyer, but this book explains the many ways we are predictably irrational. It discusses many business cases that show that people won't do what you think they might—something that's important for you to know as you're making decisions about marketing, product or service delivery, and positioning.

Influence by Richard Cialdini

This book discusses the six universal psychological principles that influence why people say yes. If you know why people say yes and apply the principles in your marketing, sales conversations, and negotiations, you'll be more likely to get a yes rather than a maybe or a no.

Create Your Own Employee Handbook by Lisa Guerin and Amy Delpo

The thought of hiring employees overwhelms so many small business owners. This book discusses the various factors to consider, and it comes with a CD containing policy templates you can adapt. If you have a question about hiring and managing employees, the book probably addresses it or shows you where to find the information you need.

QUESTIONS OR COMMENTS?

I'd love to hear your thoughts and reactions to this book. Email me at charlie@productiveflourishing.com.

Want More Small Business Resources?

I've prepared a resource page that complements this book at www.productiveflourishing.com/small-business-life-cycle/. Resources are continually being added there as I share more strategies, tips, tools, and worksheets.

Need Tailored Help?

My company helps people and businesses take meaningful action on the stuff that matters. Our sweet spot for businesses is Stages 2–4, as we're able to help businesses focus on the things that are working really well and on getting their people, processes, systems, and positioning right as they work through Stage 3. If you're interested in learning more about how we can help, check out www.ProductiveFlourishing.com/Services.

One Last Thing

I'd be honored if you'd share this book with your friends. *We need more thriving small businesses.*

In addition, I'd be very grateful if you posted a review on Amazon. Positive reviews mean more people will see and buy this book, which means we'll jointly be able to help small businesses thrive. Just go to www.amzn.com/B00C3G9F4G to leave a review.

Best,
Charlie

ACKNOWLEDGMENTS

This book would not exist were it not for the creative village I'm blessed to be a part of. I'd like to thank members of my team, past and present, who each touched this project in different ways: Marissa Bracke, Dusti Arab, Lisa Wood, Ashley Herzberger, and Sarah Lacy. Dusti, in particular, pulled this idea out of the fallow fields of content I had lying around and made it public.

There has been a team of editors, as well. Linda Dessau from ContentMasteryGuide.com edited the project and had the unenviable task of polishing rough material written and developed over the course of years into one coherent voice. Chris O'Byrne and his team at JETLAUNCH.net masterfully formatted and designed the digital and print versions of the book while shepherding it to Amazon and providing invaluable editorial insights. Catherine E. Oliver at Oliver-Editorial.com did a masterful job of line-editing the finished version and catalyzing more cogent explanations and examples.

My pack of co-mentors and teachers—Pam Slim, Jonathan Fields, Mark Silver, Michael Bungay Stanier, Seth Godin, and Les McKeown—inspired, taught, and nudged me to continue working on the project throughout its development, often without knowing they were doing so. My clients, workshop participants, customers, and readers have graciously shared their journeys with me and helped me refine the content to its simplest and most insightful form; they have been the best teachers and editors.

And, lastly, without Angela Wheeler's unconditional support, I surely would not be in the position of doing great work that matters with a community that I so deeply care about. I'm blessed to have such a wonderful wife and business partner.

Thank you all. *Ubuntu*. (I am who I am because of who we all are.)

35708056R20049